Making Medicine

For Sharla —

   Wishing you blessings from
all the animal spirits & from
the good medicines of the tao.

Respects,
David Carson

2·3·04
Arroyo Seco, N. Mex.

Also by David Carson

Medicine Cards: Revised, Expanded Edition (with Jamie Sams)

Making Medicine

A GUIDED JOURNAL FOR MEDICINE CARDS

David Carson

Illustrations by Angela Werneke

 ST. MARTIN'S GRIFFIN ᛗ NEW YORK

www.stmartins.com

Library of Congress Cataloging-in-Publication Data

Carson, David.
    Making medicine : a guided journal for Medicine cards / David Carson ; illustrations by
Angela Werneke.—1st St. Martin's Griffin ed.
        p.   cm.
    ISBN 0-312-28739-9
    1. Fortune-telling by cards.   2. Animals—Miscellanea.   3. Healing—Miscellanea.
4. Indians of North America—Miscellanea.   I. Sams, Jamie, 1951–   Medicine cards.   II. Title.
BF1878 .C28   2002
133.3'242—dc21   2001048780

First Edition: February 2002

10 9 8 7 6 5 4 3 2 1

Contents

Acknowledgments

I am grateful to thousands of people who have touched my life with light and beauty. To acknowledge all of them would be a book in itself. Know, however, that you are etched and treasured in my memory.

My very special thanks to Jamie Sams for her inspiring love of all living creatures.

The first mention of a possibility for this journal came about in a phone conversation with Susan Schulman. With all the various legal, ownership, and other hurdles I knew the book would face, I did not see how it would ever see publication. Susan did. I would like to express my gratitude for her encouragement, enthusiasm, and guidance, which was the certain genesis of the text. I bow to both her literary insights and business skills. Thanks are due to Julia Cameron, who introduced me to Susan. Also to Rhonda Flemming for her loving heart and spiritual depth.

Thanks are always due to intellectual properties attorney M. J. Bogatin.

Many thanks to the editor, Keith Kahla of St. Martin's Press, who deserves much credit where this book is concerned. And to assistant editor Teresa Theophano. To those many nameless but skillful people who I have never met at St. Martin's Press who do the day-to-day hands-on work of modern-day publishing, you also have my gratitude.

Like most people, my greatest debt is to my family. Thanks to Virginia and James Bethel, Linda and Danny Perez, and Jim and Corinne Wilson, and to Jim and Robbie Robertson for putting me on their Native American album and on the documentary. My heartfelt thanks to Nina, who helped me in all ways. And to Marta, Jason, Jacqui, Jon, and Kelly. Thanks to Sara and Greta for their direct help. To my magical twin daughters, Elizabeth and Margaret, who are spontaneity and creativity itself—a deep well of love, beauty, and joy.

About This Book

Upon this earth, there are people with great visions and great dreams. There are people who have touched the highest spiritual planes. Great teachers tell us that life is simple and beautiful. Very little is needed to lead a fulfilling existence. Life—any life, is mysterious and miraculous. In the presence of the great ones, our teachers, elders, and instructors, we feel the magic all around us, and we instinctively know there are hidden doorways to magical-mind and realized states of being.

Native American teachers have taught that there are many such doorways, many paths to the goal of truth and happiness. There are ways of dancing, singing, fasting, purifying, and praying. There are paths of the intellect and mind. There is the warrior path and paths of the Little Medicine Wheel and Big Medicine Wheel—microcosm and macrocosm. And there are numerable paths of the heart.

Eventually, all roads lead to the center. But there is no more powerful path or doorway than those doors guarded by the animal powers. It is a generally accepted fact among shamanic cultures that animals hold the key to unlock the door of personal realization and spiritual understanding. But animals are the key masters to many other gifts as well. Each animal has a gift for you.

There is a story that illustrates this.

In the beginning of this world, all creatures great and small met in a circle— the first circle of the animals. The creatures held a powwow and each animal spoke in turn so that they might learn from one another.

Eagle spoke of warrior power and the power to see the panorama of life. Prairie Dog spoke of the world above and the world below the ground. Bear spoke of the sacred dreams of winter. Swallow spoke of the swiftness of thought and powers of the darting and swooping intellect. Woolly Mammoth, Mastodon, spoke of ancestors and honoring the past. Moth spoke of Moon's beauty and flying through the gates of vision to light. Turtle spoke of the power of slowness and appreciating each step of the journey. Salmon spoke of rushing waters and how to navigate in the quest to return to the birthing place.

Hummingbird spoke of the beautiful flowers and the sweetness of life. Red Parrot spoke of listening and hearing what is really being said—the subtleties of language. Bee spoke of her buzzing mantra and of following the sound on the path of apprenticeship. Ocelot spoke of methods of tracing and tracking. Woodpecker spoke of the powers of drumming. Condor spoke of purification. Chipmunk spoke of time; she told how she carried thirteen stripes on her back, signifying the lunar months. Monarch Butterfly spoke of returning to her special trees and of dancing and celebrating the gift of life.

Monkey spoke of pranks and other mischievous deeds. Bat spoke of the friendly powers of night and how one can awaken to new life. Skunk told of how she had finally gained respect from all others. Pony told of the freedom of running over the boundless plains. Kit Fox spoke of the ability to blend into the environment and the ability to hide her true nature. Opossum merely grinned.

Each animal had a turn and they all shared their experience and knowledge. Each had a wondrous teaching—and on and on it went. Each made their individual contribution to the wheel of life. When each and every animal had spoken, Eagle said, "One is not among us—the two-legged, the human being. Humans alone have fallen from Creator's plan. Humans have forgotten how to reverence all of life, to recognize us one and all as sisters and brothers. But we can help them to realize themselves. We will be their unfailing friends and helpers.

"Our gifts we will freely share and our teachings and our medicines. We will teach humans how to live and be in right relations with all of life. We will assist them, protect them, and guide them. If they are respectful enough to recognize our gifts, we will lead them through the invisible doorway to Great Spirit."

So the story goes.

Humans have been seeking advice and the perfect understanding and cooperation that animals teach for a long time—the perfect oneness of heart, mind, body, and spirit. Animals have been shamanized since the dawn of human history for these valuable qualities. We carry these medicines within us. It is for you to discover these powers and use them to your best advantage.

Here is a scrapbook and journal to augment the use of Medicine Cards. Here is a journal of self-discovery and renewal. Use it. Use it to honor your animal spirit guides and the spirit of other animals. These pages are for you and will return to you at least as much as you put into them.

I believe that each of us is our own best teacher. To discover the power of animals we must discover ourselves, just as Eagle told it. This journal, *Making Medicine,* is a tool to help you along the way on your journey to self-understanding.

I hope you will use it and I hope it brings you joy and sweet medicine and that it comforts and teaches you on your individual path. May you always meet with truth and beauty—may truth and beauty always surround you.

David Carson
Taos, New Mexico, 2001

The Power of Animals

The understanding of animals furthers our human potential. Animals open the totality of our being. They help us to move beyond the intellect. They bring new capability and new awareness. They give us strength. This is medicine.

First, learn to make medicine for yourself. Then it's easy enough to make it for others. The following pages ask you to pay attention to the animals you meet on your path. Animals have a vast range of capabilities and skills. These pages offer a personal and more complete connection to animal medicine. It's not about self-improvement, though that might be an incidental bonus. You are who you are. Behavior—the world's measure—can always be changed. Seek essence. Seek essence so you can understand other forms of life. Use this section of the journal as a mosaic of an ever-changing puzzle that eventually fits together as a cogent whole. Record your dreams, your visions, moments when you slip beneath appearances into other levels of awareness. Be humble so that you may understand an animal's language—energy and teaching.

To use the following segment of the journal, first randomly select a Medicine Card. You may wish to reread the original Medicine Card text of the animal you have selected before you begin. You may also want to take a moment of silence to reflect on your card choice and get in touch with your higher self. Try to connect with the medicine of the animal. Try to communicate with her or him on the subtle planes. Ask for power, for medicine. Ask the animal to help you to see, to write, to understand. Ask the animal you have selected for balance and guidance on life's bumpy highway.

Once you have selected a card, find the corresponding pages for that animal in your journal. Read the suggestions underneath the shield. Then write. Do not feel as though you have to solely write. Create a poem. Feel free to draw, collage, any method to move you into a deeper kinship with the magic of animals. Use your pages to keep beautiful leaves, feathers, and other important mementos and keepsakes. If you have a dream of a certain animal, write about it in the relevant pages. You may also want to paste in pictures of spiritual teachers, sacred spaces, or power places you have visited. Be creative.

Remember to date your work. You may want to look at it sequentially at sometime in the future. Write without too much thinking. Write what is relevant to you. Throughout the entire journal, it is recommended that you write or draw whatever occurs to you even though it makes no logical sense. You may return at any time to your pages to add any new insights or thoughts you may have had.

The following portion of the journal profiling each Medicine Card is not meant to be sequential. However, it is up to you how you use it. Put animals at the center of your hoop. Try to understand our symbolic relationship to their presence and teaching over millennia of time.

You may decide to keep your journal on your altar or some other special place. You may want to create a circle. You may want to jot down a note about where the moon resides when you use your journal. Her face, in all aspects, provides the human with an observable series of rhythms—rhythm upon rhythm. Use her for structure. This scrapbook and journal can be a ceremony. Cermonies do not have to be complicated. Your body is a tree—the tree of life. Your heartbeat is a drum. Your breath is a song. You are a living creature within the ceremony of life—the life of all beings.

Only you can bring your unique experiences to these pages in the act of creative self-expression.

GUIDED JOURNAL

O
Lightning

ILLUMINATION

Use the power of Lightning to find inner guidance. Do not be discouraged by life's difficulties. Lightning counsels you to remember there is a divine spark within. That spark can burst forth as a blinding light. Allow this to happen. Bring forth your own true light which can have an incalculable effect on illuminating your situation. Use the journal pages to record any insights or flashes of inspiration you may have.

Listen to the thunder, the powerful chant of the Red Shaman.

Be heard, be respected, and be believed. Make a terrible noise if you have to.

*Lightning is a
gift from
the eye of
Thunderbeing.*

*Lightning is
violent. It
changes and
transforms.*

*With
Lightning,
you are being
given fire
energy from
the pure
diamond of
the inner
self.*

1
Eagle
SPIRIT

Before Lord Krishna, before Buddha, before Jesus, there was Eagle. Eagle asks about your relationship to Great Mystery. In the following pages, explore your deepest spiritual beliefs. Write about your spiritual guides and teachers, your way or spiritual philosophy, your understandings and insights. How do you touch with the divine?

For eons, Eagle has soared high over Turtle Island.

Great Mystery said to Eagle, "Go and teach them the sacred flight of spirit."

*Through
eagle, one's
place in the
cosmos
becomes
clear.*

_Eagle
medicine
gives our
spirit flight.
Let it fly._

*Eagle frees
us, leading
us up to
boundless
spirit.*

2
Hawk

MESSENGER

The art of communication is the secret of secrets and Hawk is the messenger. Much of medicine is about listening, sharpening your ears in order to translate the communication arriving from other planes and from other entities. Write about your communication skills and how you might improve them. If you have a message for someone who isn't listening, consider new ways to get it across.

*Hawk holds
a message
for you.*

Hawk penetrates the veil of confusion between the worlds and opens the heart of the attuned listener.

If you are making noise, internally or externally, you will not be able to hear Hawk's advise.

_You may
have a
message
about your
inner attitude
right in front
of you._

*Communicate
clearly so
your own
message
can be
understood.*

3
Elk

STAMINA

Elk teaches the wise use of energy, how to overcome stress and go the distance.
Call upon this medicine whenever you have an arduous task that takes a long
time. Time each action to fit the situation. What gives you strength and stamina?
What can you do to increase your energy levels? Examine your diet. Perhaps you
can begin a program of exercise. Use your journal to formulate a plan to increase
stamina and record your progress.

Elk sets the pace.

This may be the time to undertake a long-term project.

*Utilize
energy
wisely.*

_Pacing
yourself will
allow you
to go much
farther._

*Stamina is
more than
the ability
to last. It is
the ability to
prevail.*

4
Deer

GENTLENESS

Deer counsels you to gentle down easy. No need to fuss and fight. Deer has a heightened state of awareness and is associated with the path of the heart. She typifies the walk of love and compassion. This is a good place to write about matters of the heart. Who and what are your loves? Discuss them in detail. Do your loves awaken your gentleness of spirit?

In the bustle of everyday life you may find yourself responding in kind. "First, slowly, slowly," Deer counsels. "Find gentleness within. Then you may go swiftly."

_Call upon
your own
gentleness in
the interest of
healing._

222

Deer can bestow on you soft and quieted medicine eyes—eyes of compassion with which to see the spirits of the animals.

Compassion and gentleness walk hand in hand. Put away anger and fear. Compassion is a higher expression of spiritual development.

*Look into
your own
heart for the
love you hold
for yourself.
Compassion
flows from
this to others.*

5
Bear

INTROSPECTION

She is the left-handed magician who keeps the inner territories. She teaches introspection. Knowledge gained by introspection needs time and is a step by step progression. You need deep inner discipline. Treading the inner planes is the essence of true understanding. Culture traps one in the game of self-importance, but Bear sets us free. What is your method to go inside yourself and learn your personal truth? Where is your cave? Discuss in your journal what you have gleaned from going within.

What part of
your time is
spent in
introspection?

_____
_____
_____
_____
_____
_____
_____
_____
_____
_____
_____
_____
_____
_____
_____
_____
_____
_____
_____
_____
_____
_____
_____
_____
_____
_____
_____
_____
_____
_____
_____
_____

Bear is our closest relation.

*Bear goes
into her cave
to possess the
spiritual sky.*

_When Bear
emerges from
her cave, her
path is clear._

*Bear is a
hibernator.
She says,
"Meditate,
reflect, move
within."*

6
Snake

TRANSMUTATION

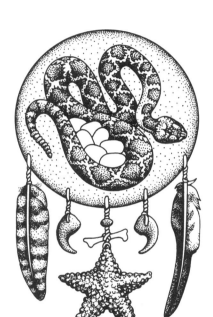

She is the alchemist. Most people fear snakes but Snake is a wise teacher. She knows that matter has different qualities and different densities. She teaches perfect balance, how to transmute one state of matter to another. She teaches how to work miracles and bring healing into our lives. Use your journal to draw a circle of self and situation. Draw a circle that represents you. Write inside of the circle a description of your present situation. Imagine you have the power of Snake to coil and wrap yourself around your situation and transmute it. Write any new insight about what you can do to shift struggle or strife and bring it into balance and harmony.

*Snake brings
great healing
and
restorative
force.*

Like Snake,
it is often
necessary to
move in,
over, under,
and through
a situation.

*Snake asks
you to shed
your skin so
that another
can replace it.
Be less
resistant to
change.*

_____
_____
_____
_____
_____
_____
_____
_____
_____
_____
_____
_____
_____
_____
_____
_____
_____
_____
_____
_____
_____
_____
_____
_____
_____
_____
_____
_____
_____
_____
_____
_____
_____
_____
_____
_____
_____

Snake represents the umbilical cord attached to the placenta of spirit.

Serpent power gives you the ability to strike.

7
skunk

REPUTATION

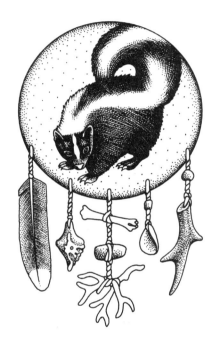

Native America is a respectful culture. The People have respect for the environment, animals, children, and elders. Use your journal to reflect upon issues of status. How do people see you and how do you wish to be perceived? Do you respect people out of fear or because of their accomplishments? Who do you most respect? What can you do to gain the respect of others, and why do you care?

What are your thoughts about your own reputation?

_Skunk has
earned a big
reputation._

*Respect
fosters
respect.*

_A good
reputation,
once lost, is
difficult to
regain._

*The loss of
self-respect is
always a
tragedy.*

8
Otter

WOMAN MEDICINE

Otter keeps many mothering powers. She makes no mistakes because her understanding is limitless. Imagine the female as an adept—completely at one with her
environment and able to swim through the spiritual realms because of her magical nature. Close your eyes and see a creature who represents the female within
you. Describe her. Ask her for a message, an image, a word. Write about woman
power and Otter's meaning to you.

Otter offers you the freedom to live a life for which you are best suited.

No guile, no
judgment.
Be open.
Get in the
swim of life
and love it.

Look at your
feminine side
to assess
health and
well-being.

Receptivity allows us to enjoy our lives much more fully.

*Otter wants
you to be
happy and
ready to
play.*

9
Butterfly

TRANSFORMATION

Where are you on the Butterfly Wheel? Are you an egg? Caterpillar? Chrysalis? Emerged Butterfly? What is transforming in your life? Who are you becoming with the passing of life's seasons? What situation or pattern would you like to transform? Write about the transformation process. Call on Butterfly to speed it along and for the best results.

Butterfly is a
great warrior
related to the
Sun—flitting
and darting—
impossible to
predict.

Butterfly can help you achieve a lightness of spirit as no other medicine can.

*Your very
dance around
the tree of life
is Butterfly's
gift.*

*Butterfly's
path is the
beauty road.*

*Butterfly
knows the
Sacred
Tree, the
Remembering
Tree, the Tree
of the People.*

10
Turtle

MOTHER EARTH

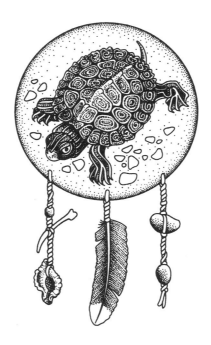

What are your thoughts about Turtle medicine? How are you related to Mother Earth? Describe this relationship. Day and night the waters flow over the face of our Mother. Your body is a map. Where do you locate the forces that flow through your creativity? Create some images that describe you. Sum up this process in your journal.

Turtle
reminds us
that we are
always at
home.

_Acknowledge
your
connection to
Mother
Earth._

"*I carry a great island on my back,*" *says Turtle. "I am strong and live to be old like the Earth.*"

_____
_____
_____
_____
_____
_____
_____
_____
_____
_____
_____
_____
_____
_____
_____
_____
_____
_____
_____
_____
_____
_____
_____
_____
_____
_____
_____
_____
_____
_____
_____
_____
_____
_____
_____
_____

Turtle, with its slow, sure steps, wins the race.

*Turtle
teaches about
the Sacred
Mother from
which we
come, the
Earth that
holds the
spirit of our
Holy
Ancestors.*

11
Moose

SELF-ESTEEM

Self-love. Self-esteem. Do you have them? Are you proud to be who you are? Use your journal to discuss how you feel about yourself. Without self-love we have no center from which to love others. List your accomplishments. Praise yourself and allow yourself the freedom to write yourself a long, moving, love letter.

*True
self-esteem
has no need
to be
boastful.*

_____
_____
_____
_____
_____
_____
_____
_____
_____
_____
_____
_____
_____
_____
_____
_____
_____
_____
_____
_____
_____
_____
_____
_____
_____
_____
_____
_____
_____
_____
_____

Self-esteem is not swollen pride, which will burst. True self-esteem is our birthright.

*Never
apologize for
who you are.*

Self-esteem is
not the ego.
It is the
essence of
spirit.

Consciousness.
This is
self-esteem.

12
Porcupine

INNOCENCE

Porcupine has the medicine of purest innocence because she has so few enemies. She lives in the south on the Medicine Wheel. The innocent willingly falls back-wards into the arms of Great Mystery because she knows how to trust. Where do you stand with this medicine? Can you write about the times when you gained worldly knowledge? What has shocked you lately? Speculate about the quality of your present innocence.

Innocence is not callused, but it can be sharp.

It is the playground laughter of children on a summer evening.

*Great
Mystery gave
Porcupine
her place in
the world.
"Walk your
road in
innocence,"
Great
Mystery
said.*

The Little People, the spirit medicine of the forest— they come running to help the innocent.

*The child
unpacks the
world. Each
thing, the
metamorphosis
of spring.*

13
Coyote

TRICKSTER

Coyote felt in his medicine bag for the small bottle of Scotch. Coyote slipped quietly into the wrong apartment. "I'm really hungry. I wonder if I can eat this cactus?" Coyote says. Painful episodes are a way of life for Coyote, yet Coyote's medicine is full of mirth and laughter. Coyote reminds us not to make assumptions least our adventure become misadventure. There may be complications or details you have not considered. What is the most embarrassing incident in your life and how was it resolved? Write about painful mistakes. Extrapolate lessons from them.

Old hungry,
hurry-up
Coyote,
scares away
the game.

*Once I saw a
Coyote. It
looked kinda
like you.*

Coyote took off his mask. "Dang! I'm still a coyote!" he exclaimed.

It's not a good idea to play follow the leader when the leader is Coyote.

Coyote pays three times as much for the designer label ACME.

14
Dog

LOYALTY

Here are questions of loyalty. Who or what are you loyal to and what are you willing to fight for, or even to die for? What do you stand guard and watch over and protect? Do you have conflicting loyalties? Here is the place to hash them out. This is the place in your journal to make sure you know and understand your loyalties. Develop clarity about your loyalties so you can internalize and act upon them without question.

*A Dog
soldier serves
the People.*

_____
_____
_____
_____
_____
_____
_____
_____
_____
_____
_____
_____
_____
_____
_____
_____
_____
_____
_____
_____
_____
_____
_____
_____
_____
_____
_____
_____
_____
_____
_____
_____
_____
_____
_____
_____

Do you feel the protection of Dog's medicine in both your inner and outer worlds?

Ask Dog to protect your sacred space.

Dog has always been loyal to humans who show they are worthy of loyalty.

Romping,
jumping,
playing,
growling, and
barking—
exuberance
is a gift
from Dog.
Receive it.

15
Wolf

TEACHER

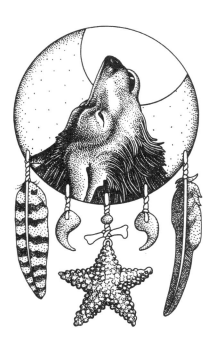

Ask the pathfinder to guide you on the learning road. Here you might wish to write about significant teachers you have had. Write about school experiences both good and bad. How do you view education? Who is your ideal teacher? How do you awaken the teacher within? What is it that you have to teach? What is your educational background? What have you gained or lost by it? What do you teach and exemplify by your behavior? What do you want to learn? Light the fire in your wolf lodge. Make plans to achieve your learning goals.

*When Wolf
finds herself
alone, she
offers prayers
to the void.*

Wolf is often the teacher of measure and order. She knows all the trails of this round Earth.

Wolf says, "Take a dare. Challenge belief. Push beyond habit and comfort. Enlarge experience. Thus begins the learning path."

_An authentic
teacher is a
transformer._

*Tracking into
the realm
where
questions and
answers
coexist, Wolf
teaches that
the brain is
not the lodge
of wisdom,
Eternity is.*

16
Raven

MAGIC

Raven asks our responsibility to magic. Are you willing to don the black cloak of the magician? We can all be magical for someone. Write about magic. Tell about the magical events you have encountered. Tell about magical people in your life. Tell about the magic you have been able to share with others—perhaps a special someone.

*Don't dwell
upon magic
lest you
chase it
away.*

_____
_____
_____
_____
_____
_____
_____
_____
_____
_____
_____
_____
_____
_____
_____
_____
_____
_____
_____
_____
_____
_____
_____
_____
_____
_____
_____
_____
_____
_____
_____
_____
_____
_____

*Raven
symbolizes
the medicine
of magic.
Raven also
brings it.
Raven is the
magician.*

GUIDED JOURNAL 102

*Be aware of
the magic
which is
around you.*

Do not be afraid to step into the magician's circle. Magic becomes you.

Abracadabra,
Raven
appears.
Abracadabra,
Raven
vanishes.

17
Mountain Lion

LEADERSHIP

True leaders are willing, strong, deserving, and compassionate. What are the conditions of the relationship between you and those in your charge or those in charge of you? Do you have natural qualities to assume the role of leader? Are you willing to take the responsibility of being chief? Do you trust authority? What is the legacy your leaders have left you? What will you leave those who follow? You may want to use these pages to discuss and come to terms with these ideas.

Leaders must
first go up
on the
mountain.

All the truly great leaders of this world have led by example.

A true leader does not imprison you. A true leader tells you to use your own judgment.

Leadership is an attitude—a way that never violates others.

In the old way, a leader walked behind the people— Walks Last—and helped the people with their burdens.

18
Lynx

SECRETS

Lynx is seldom seen. To cast one's eye on Lynx is good medicine. Lynx keeps to herself—alone with the secrets of the ages. Her gait is luxuriant and sleek. She has crossed the starry path and has been to the summit of the universe. She knows secrets. You may want to use Lynx medicine to try to fathom the secrets of others. You may want to use it to see what you are keeping secret from yourself. Now is the time to come clean. Write down the secrets you are keeping. You can always erase them.

A Lynx
person makes
you feel as if
you have
been
X-rayed.

*What is your
secret and
why is it so?*

"Why did you hide from Creator's love?" Lynx asks. "Find this secret within yourself and you will have my medicine."

Lynx has seen Great Mystery, a light greater than a million suns. That is why Lynx's eyes squint even to this day.

Lynx painted a map of the starry path on her pelt leading to Great Mystery. This is the reason why Lynx will never forget the way.

19
Buffalo

PRAYER & ABUNDANCE

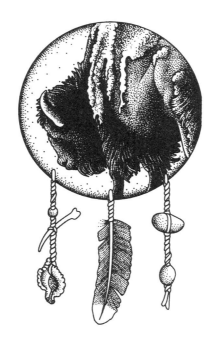

Do you feel gratitude for what you have? What are your beliefs about the material world and abundance? Do you honor your relatives? Not simply human relatives but the many kinds of dirts, campfires, winds, rains, waters, manifestations, mountains, forests, plants, and animals? Do you honor the ancestors who struggled so hard to make a place for you in the generations to come? Use your journal to reflect on abundance. Express your gratitude to Great Mystery for giving you life and the means to continue it. Here is the place to create your deepest and most heartfelt prayer—to let your breath be lifted to Great Mystery's breath.

*See the
abundance
all around
you.*

Buffalo is
sacred.
Buffalo is
food for
spirit.

Walk with Buffalo and your needs will be met.

_Like the
shell game,
the spiritual
is hidden
inside the
material.
Don't fail to
appreciate it._

Buffalo offered the human its life, meat, skin, horn, bone. What is your gift?

20
Mouse

SCRUTINY

Mouse teaches that there is power in little things. Mouse touches everything with its whiskers and looks up close. Mouse counsels you to deal with minutiae. Pay close attention to details. Chew it to pieces. Sort it out. Systematize it. Make it accessible. This is good advice. What tiny stuff are you forgetting? Are you dotting the I and crossing the T? What little things do you enjoy doing that give you a feeling of accomplishment? What is some little thing you can do to make you or someone else feel better? Here is the place in your journal to discuss your little joys and sorrows. Find the seeds of happiness. Perhaps they will sprout and become huge.

*Mouse
medicine
requires
presence,
awareness,
and attention.*

*Pay close
attention
now.*

*Seek to
know each
component of
the greater
whole.*

Scrutiny isn't limited to just the eyes. All our senses come into play.

*Focus now.
Little things
add up to
big ones.*

21
Owl

DECEPTION

Owl loves the night and the chase. Owl teaches us to see in the dark and to listen to the subtleties of cloaked language. Remember that owl's feathers grow
darkest where they receive the most light. Owl's feathers are called deceiver
feathers. When and by whom have you been deceived? What do you think is
your greatest self-deception? How can Owl medicine help you to see the truth?
Are you afraid of Owl or can Owl be an ally to assist you in finding out what is
hidden in the dark? Take your journal writing into the half-light that you mis-
take for darkness and see what revelations come to you.

*If things
don't feel
right, ask the
spirit of Owl
to interpret
for you.*

_Owl is a
clairvoyant
and a master
of subjective
dimensions._

Owl teaches
that we
always know
when we
are being
deceived. She
shows us our
agreement on
a deep level.

_Owl people
see far
beyond
perception,
which is
often
deception._

An Owl person is not always a black sorcerer. Sometimes they are snowy white.

22
Beaver

BUILDER

Beaver tells us to have the right tools to do the job right. Grandmother Two Teeth knows the art of building and architecture. This can also mean the architecture of your life. What are you building? What are your goals and ambitions and how are you manifesting them? If you don't have a master plan, use these journal pages to develop one. Read it out loud four times a day for four days. Get comfortable with it. Then activate it. Keep notes on your progress.

Beaver's colony is a matriarchy. Females lead.

_Beaver never
regrets the
hectic pace
of her life.
She is the
quintessence
of growth._

*The wisdom
of Beaver is
that she gets
the work
done.*

Beaver's magic is that she constructs so well on the inner planes. The material achievement follows.

Of course,
Great Spirit
is the Master
Builder.
Beaver runs
a close
second.

23
Opossum

DIVERSION

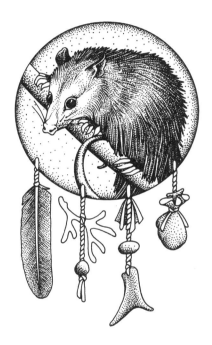

Opossum wraps his tail around a tree branch and hangs upside-down. This is an unfamiliar position, a contrary position. The medicine often gives you a glimpse of the inverse, the wellsprings of our consciousness. Here's your journal opportunity to look carefully at your diversions, distractions, and digressions. Leave the main current and take a different trail. It's a chance to hang upside down verbally. Opossum often moves to a new den. Write about the times that you have used Opossum's strategy. When have you left your trail to explore something totally different and what were the results?

*Do more
than
examine a
personal
pattern.
Turn it
inside out.*

_Opossum
medicine
allows
insights to
bubble up
from our
unconscious._

*If you are
stymied, try
playing dead.
This is the
way of the
Opossum.*

Turn your life around. Opossum often suggests a new path in order to bring a change to your situation.

*Are you
uninspired?
Opossum
offers many
alternatives.*

24
Crow

LAW

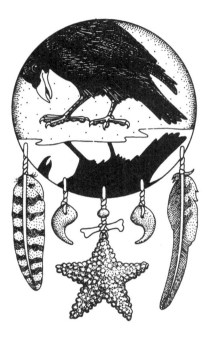

Crow sees many worlds and knows the laws of all of them. No one knows the shadow world as crow does. The shadow hides the true self shrouded in its oc-cluded depths. What are your thoughts about shadow? What is law and what is judgment? What are your beliefs about justice? What are your thoughts about spiritual law and earthly law? What is the highest law? What eggs are hatching from the nest of your Shadowland? These are some of the questions you may want to explore when considering Crow medicine.

*Change is
the law.
Nothing is
fixed in
time.*

Crow
understands
the void.

Man's law is like a treaty—created to be broken and sent up in smoke. Spiritual law is forever.

_Look closely
at the laws
you have
established
for yourself.
Which ones
are relevant?_

Do not deny the law. It is the shining path that cuts through shadows.

25
Fox

CAMOUFLAGE

Fox has been blessed with the ability to conceal or blend-in when the need arises. She teaches you the same ability. No one can harm you if you are not there. Have you developed your art of camouflage? How often have you been out-foxed and drawn into a dangerous situation? Discuss your own methods of camouflage. Are they effective? How can you further this ability?

*Fox teaches
the tracker
the fox
trot—the
way of
invisibility.*

People rarely see Fox in the cities, although many live there.

*Learn Fox's
crafty lesson
and be
invisible. Be
seen when
and how you
choose.*

Mind can
never figure
out Fox's
medicine.
To learn it,
ask your
conscious
mind not to
interfere.

*Foxiness is
an attitude.*

26
Squirrel

GATHERING

Squirrel teaches humans how to squirrel away but not to hoard. Squirrels are willing to share with you if you are not greedy. Take some of their hard-earned resources. Do you have your provisions socked-in? List what you need to squirrel away so that it is available to you when you need it. What is your relationship to the material world? List a dozen things that nurture you. Bring them into your life. List things you need to be rid of. Give them to someone who needs them.

Squirrel
knows the
seasons. She
does not
tarry before
the onset of
winter.

_Do you have
what you
need? "Get
it," Squirrel
says._

*Be ready for
today and
plan for the
future.*

*Remember
that Squirrel
travels the
tree trails.
Squirrel loves
trees and
knows the
sacred
language
trees speak.*

*Squirrel
has a
communication
network. She
is always on
top of the
news.*

27
Dragonfly

ILLUSION

Simple. It's all in the mind. Dragonfly is the master of illusion, able to juggle and reflect light in marvelous ways. The medicine of illusion is more than tromp l'oeil, simply fooling the eye. Dragonfly blurs perceptions and brings one into a world outside of time and space—a world of intoxicating colors. Shimmering. Iridescent. Beautiful. But see through appearances. Use the pages to consider illusion—maya. Use Dragonfly medicine to create your own illusions. Consider ways to bring a myriad of colors and sparkling lights into your living space.

Few of us
would deny
that there is
a light
spectrum
above and
below our
ability to see.
Be willing to
seek the
unseen.

_Dragonfly's
thin wings
carry
jewellike
worlds of
wondrous
beauty._

*Existence is
the blurred
flight of an
arrow.*

Don't be destroyed by illusion.

The power to create illusion is an art form.

28
Armadillo

BOUNDARIES

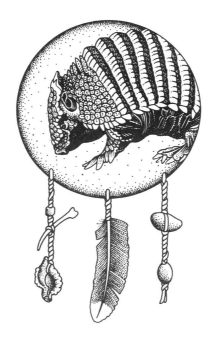

Armadillo is often called "Shield Carrier." Armadillo has set and secure boundaries. She asks how you can shield yourself, your family, your possessions, your home. What boundaries are you expressing and holding? Are your boundaries limiting you or protecting you? Meditate on a shield in each direction, an East shield, a South shield, a West shield, a North shield, and a central shield. These shields protect different aspects of an individual. How might you effectively use each shield for your own protection? Use these pages to reexamine your boundaries. Use these pages to destroy old shields and give birth to new, more appropriate ones.

Armadillo's challenge is to oppose detrimental forces from the outside. She shows you how to build your spirit fence.

What boundaries do you express in different situations?

*If you have
an objective
that meets
with much
opposition,
call on
Armadillo,
the Shield
Carrier, for
her protection
and help.*

_____
_____
_____
_____
_____
_____
_____
_____
_____
_____
_____
_____
_____
_____
_____
_____
_____
_____
_____
_____
_____
_____
_____
_____
_____
_____
_____
_____
_____
_____
_____
_____
_____

Use Armadillo medicine for protection when you are traveling to dangerous places. There is no better medicine than this one.

Are you
afraid to
expose your
sensitive
nature?
Perhaps now
is the time to
remove your
armor.

29
Badger

AGGRESSIVENESS

Badger is fearless, tenacious, and ferocious. He will use male warrior energy to meet any challenge, and he will never wave the white flag of surrender. Aggression may make you feel powerful, but it is also limiting, like a cage, as it narrows possibility. A principle of martial arts is to acquiesce to the opponent's aggression. Allow it to defeat itself. Under what circumstances have you been able to do this? Are your aggressive tendencies harming or helping you in the long campaign? If you must fight, use Badger's medicine wisely. Aggression begets aggression. But don't let anyone tell you not to fight when necessary. Aggression can be positive. Let Badger's medicine show you the way to self-assertiveness when the need arises. Use the journal pages to reflect upon your own aggressive nature. How can you use aggression more effectively and creatively?

Since Badger knows what's inside the Earth, he is on friendly terms with the underworld. He knows the medicine roots and how to use them in miraculous ways.

Fight for
your life.
You're
worth it.

*He who
hesitates is
not a
Badger.*

Badger is the
bold one and
strikes out.
He teaches
us to begin
our projects
with
boldness.

There is a time for a sharp knife and a time for a dull one.

30
Rabbit

FEAR

Here is a good place to list your fears. What is the worst thing that could happen to you? Calling down your fears is a negative aspect of creative visualization. Are you manifesting your fear? If so, how can you master it? How has your life been shaped by fear and how can you reprocess your fears? Let Rabbit show the road to courage. Use these pages to meet and face your fears.

*What you
call is what
you get.
With Rabbit
it's, "Sorry,
wrong number."*

Rabbit is a trickster. Rabbit's biggest trick is bringing fear into being.

*Don't dwell
on it.*

_____
_____
_____
_____
_____
_____
_____
_____
_____
_____
_____
_____
_____
_____
_____
_____
_____
_____
_____
_____
_____
_____
_____
_____
_____
_____
_____
_____
_____
_____
_____

Friend Rabbit teaches how to manifest through thought forms.

*When you
fear yourself,
you plot
against an
irresistible
force.*

31
Turkey

GIVE AWAY

Turkey teaches us to share our gifts. She is humble. She knows that we own nothing. All is a gift from Great Mystery. Do you care for others? Do you have a generous, giving nature? Do you make money or other offerings to show your gratitude for your many blessings? Do you give without expectations in order to know the joy of true giving? Do you give too much? Too little? Turkey will assist you in attaining a balance in the give and take of life. Give to others but gift yourself as well. Write about your personal give-aways. What are your gifts? How are you sharing them?

*Turkey
people know
how to share.
That's the
magic of their
medicine.*

Certain ancient cultures raised turkeys for their vigilant medicine eye and their medicine powers of divination. These turkeys died of old age and natural causes. To kill them was bad medicine.

*Give a gift to
a friend.*

_____
_____
_____
_____
_____
_____
_____
_____
_____
_____
_____
_____
_____
_____
_____
_____
_____
_____
_____
_____
_____
_____
_____
_____
_____
_____
_____
_____
_____
_____
_____
_____

Gratitude is the foundation from which a gift is given.

What you give is what you get.

32
Ant

PATIENCE

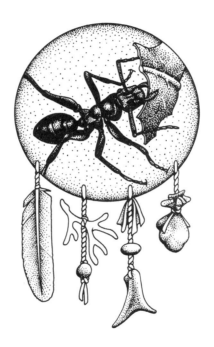

Ant does not fight with himself over things that must be done, yet Ant's work is never done. Everyone can profit from the lessons and medicines of Ant. Ant teaches hard work and patience to complete your obligation or project. Listen carefully to your Ant medicine. Think about your "workplace" and your contribution to it. Here is where to examine your job, your occupation, your life's tasks, your mission. Look at your dissatisfactions. Look at your occupational struggles. How can you help yourself to make it better? What are your thoughts, feelings, and beliefs about work and how can Ant medicine be of benefit to you?

Choose Ant
medicine to
lead you
from chaos to
order. Ant
creates
harmony
through hard
work.

_____

_____

_____

_____

_____

_____

_____

_____

_____

_____

_____

_____

_____

_____

_____

_____

_____

_____

_____

_____

_____

_____

_____

_____

_____

_____

_____

_____

_____

_____

_____

_____

_____

Patience wins the day. Use it to expend the least amount of energy.

If you have
patience in
hunting, the
game will
sense this
and be
drawn to
you.

It's easy to find Ant. Look up there on the hill.

*People who
try our
patience are
often our
best teachers.*

33
Weasel

STEALTH

Weasel will slip past you unnoticed. Stealthy Weasel knows precisely when to act, and does so with precision, but only after digesting the known facts. Learn to be quick, silent, and strong. This is the way of Weasel. How can you apply Weasel's teachings to your own situation? Do you have all the facts you need? Perhaps you should list what you know and what you don't know. Let Weasel help you get in there and ferret out what you need.

*You want
the data?
Imagine how
Weasel
might go
about
getting it.*

_____
_____
_____
_____
_____
_____
_____
_____
_____
_____
_____
_____
_____
_____
_____
_____
_____
_____
_____
_____
_____
_____
_____
_____
_____
_____
_____
_____
_____
_____
_____
_____
_____
_____

Weasel knows how to smoke out the situation in order to understand it.

The shrewd,
stealthy
Weasel
strikes again!

_____
_____
_____
_____
_____
_____
_____
_____
_____
_____
_____
_____
_____
_____
_____
_____
_____
_____
_____
_____
_____
_____
_____
_____
_____
_____
_____
_____
_____
_____
_____
_____

Learn Weasel medicine so that you can sneak down the blind alleys until you find the right one.

Weasel says, "Cut to the chase. Be silent. Be deadly. Get what you want. I do."

34
Grouse

SACRED SPIRAL

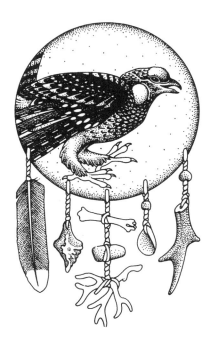

"To make Great Mystery laugh, state your plans," is an old Native American joke. Grouse asks you to consider Creator's plan for you. To enter the spiral labyrinth is to embark upon the trail of true knowledge. Entry is gained when one is willing to pass beyond preconceived notions. Grouse teaches not about your will, but a higher will than your own. Spiraling in and spiraling out creates a double helix. This is the encoding of your flesh. What is the encoding of your spirit? Where are you within the cosmic vortex? What is your understanding about this medicine?

*Grouse
teaches
lucidity.*

When we enter the sacred spiral we acknowledge Creator's plan.

To walk the mystic spiral is to tread the winding stairs of male and female power.

_It comes
and it goes,
eternally
coming and
eternally
going._

*Movement
into the
sacred spiral
unlocks a
closed mind.*

35
Horse

POWER

Horse is the Medicine Dog and represents a leap in human evolution. Black Elk's vision held many horses—medicine power from each of the four directions. Horse can be a true ally. Horse will take you there. Horse will carry your burdens. Horse expresses vital force, life itself. Horse asks you to take a look at your feelings and understanding about power. What are your issues around the concept of power? What is Horse's language to you? Tell of your own experiences with Horse. Horse reminds us not to be afraid to become powerful. Use your journal to look at the different talents, facets, and aspects of Horse.

First you
must tame
and harness
power, then
you can ride
like the
wind.

The magical medicine dog, Horse, is a mighty benefactor.

Horse can
jump you
over the
barricade—
effortlessly.

Horse reminds us we are never helpless. We can always call on Higher Power.

*Horse leads
you to an
understanding
of the nature
of power.*

36
Lizard

DREAMING

Lizard teaches that our "free soul" separates from the "body soul" during dreams and may then journey to all dimensions. There are ordinary or process dreams. There are wishing dreams. Wish dreams are manifestations of our desires, hopes, and prayers. Then there are medicine dreams which are teaching dreams charged with great spiritual purpose. Lastly, and with the most supernatural power, there are visionary dreams which are a direct meeting with ultimate personal possibility. What are your dreams teaching? Begin keeping a dream journal.

*Dreams
inform life
with meaning
and purpose.
Only the
dreamer can
make it real.*

_Lizard
teaches to
keep your
dream close
to your
heart._

If you dream about an animal four times, the animal can be your guide in meditation or dream work.

Dreams
bless our
consciousness.
And some
dreams are
spirit roads.

*Dreams have
a kinship
with death.
They teach
about the
world to
come.
In the dream
lodges we can
meet with
our ancestors.
This is holy.*

37
Antelope

ACTION

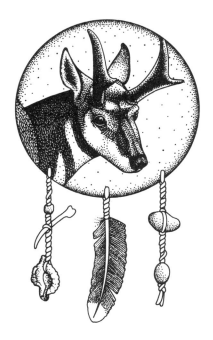

Do you exemplify the active principle or are you often in a dormant, frozen re-lationship to life? Antelope teaches quick, decisive action. Decide to decide. De-cide. Then leap into action like the Antelope. List a number of things you can achieve by engaging life and doing what is necessary. List ways to be motivated and energized. Action often leads to more action. Use your journal to become clear about your activities and the proper uses of action.

Do what is
necessary to
achieve your
goals. Do
it now.

*You don't sit
for hours and
contemplate
starting a
fire. You
light it or
you freeze.*

*Action often
brings clarity.*

Get going.
Grab hold.
Do it.

*Prioritize
your desires.
Then take
the first step.*

38
Frog

CLEANSING

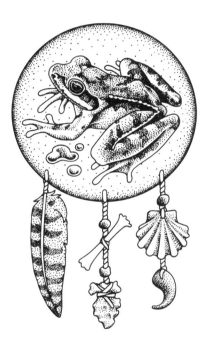

Toxicity is what will not process—from heavy metals to dead relationships. Dealing with toxicity is Frog's specialty. Frog is the bringer of rain, which cleanses Earth. What sort of cleansing is due in your life? Frog suggests you should get with it—clean up your house, your car, your physical body, or anything else that needs cleansing. Look at your emotions. Are they bound up in constraints and repression or are you in a constant upheaval and crisis? Here is the place in your journal to sort out, scrub up, and repack your emotional baggage. Here is the place to put out your garbage and empty your trash.

*Frog refreshes
us with the
feeling of a
clean, new
beginning.*

Frog asks a direct question: "Will you clean up your act on every level?"

*Bring
cleansing
into your
way of life.*

_____
_____
_____
_____
_____
_____
_____
_____
_____
_____
_____
_____
_____
_____
_____
_____
_____
_____
_____
_____
_____
_____
_____
_____
_____
_____
_____
_____
_____

Frog keeps the medicine waters—the waters of spirit.

*What makes
you feel
refreshed?*

39
Swan

GRACE

When you think of yourself, what sort of mental picture do you have? Do you carry yourself with grace in your mind's eye? Swan teaches that grace within reflects outward into the world. What do you see in your lake mirror? What can you do to realize the beauty reflecting from you? Do you seek elegance and refinement, grandeur and dignity? Are your thoughts elevated and of the highest nature? Let Swan lead you to a nobility of spirit.

*In the story
of Swan,
beauty was
born from
ugliness,
grace from
the ungainly.*

Walk in beauty. Go in grace.

*In her grace,
Swan teaches
the noble
nature of
the moment.*

_____
_____
_____
_____
_____
_____
_____
_____
_____
_____
_____
_____
_____
_____
_____
_____
_____
_____
_____
_____
_____
_____
_____
_____
_____
_____
_____
_____
_____
_____
_____
_____

Swan flies even higher than Eagle. Swan is a great shamaness because she sees not only this world but also into the next one.

*Through
movement,
Swan is
conscious of
stillness.*

40
Dolphin

MANNA

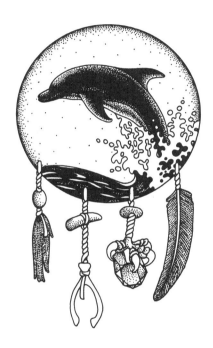

Dolphin has many medicines and is a prophetic seer. She teaches how to bring manna into your life. Manna is pure primal energy. Manna is gained through controlled breathing. Breath addresses the element of air. Great Mystery is often called "Master of Breath." First we breathe. Then we begin to understand that we are being breathed. Our life ends on the great breath of trust. Many spiritual traditions teach us to understand and use our breathing for health, happiness, and enlightenment to create personal manna. Can you describe ways to do this?

Creator blew
upon us and
our spirits
were formed.

*With our
prayers, the
visible breath
from the pipe
rises to
Creator.*

Air is the element. Because of breath, all creatures are bound together.

"We are giving you a part of our breath," the animals told the medicine people. "Go and blow our breath upon the sick in order to heal them."

*Our last
breath unites
us with
Creator.*

41
whale

RECORD KEEPER

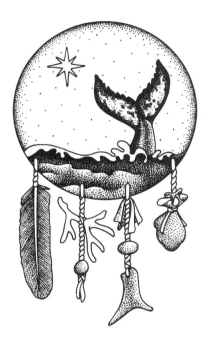

The ocean is the origin of life on this planet. Whale carries the knowledge of how life came to be. Often called Wolf-of-the-Waters, Whale keeps the record of planetary history. You can do the same. Examine all the records it is necessary for you to keep. Organize them. Here is the place for the beautiful history of your world. Perhaps you will want to draw a family tree or sing the song that only you can sing.

Whale keeps
the records.
She sings
these records
in Earth's
original
language.

*Life is a
sacred
memory.*

*Keep records
but don't
keep score.*

Only those
with a pure
heart can
understand
Whale's
song.

*To commune
with Whale
is to revisit
our past.
Consult with
this oceanic
knowledge
when
necessary.*

42
Bat

REBIRTH

Death and spirituality are entwined. Life is full of little deaths on our walk upon the Black Road of Destruction. The Black Road goes from East to West. The Red Road of Spirit goes from South to North and intersects the Black Road at the center of the Medicine Wheel. There are many animal wheels. There is a continuum beyond life—those hidden campgrounds on the other side, the land of no-fires. Bat teaches the Death Wheel. In the East is the death of an infant. In the South is the death of a child. In the West is the death of an adult. In the North is the death of an elder. And in the center, is self-death. How can you make death your ally? What are your thoughts about death? Rebirth? Ancestors? What are your fears concerning death? Can a part of the self die and another be reborn? Consider in these pages your true feelings about death and rebirth.

*Bat is a
harbinger of
new birth
and new
beginnings.*

*Don't worry.
Death comes
at the very
last minute.*

Bat medicine
is like being
given a new
bow and
new arrows
with which
to hunt.
Rebirth is the
revitalizing
death.

_____

_____

_____

_____

_____

_____

_____

_____

_____

_____

_____

_____

_____

_____

_____

_____

_____

_____

_____

_____

_____

_____

_____

_____

_____

_____

_____

_____

_____

_____

Bat medicine is a continuous festivity. You fly out of the cave every night at dusk and return at dawn.

Go deep
inside your
personal cave
in order to
encounter
eternity.

43
Spider

WEAVING

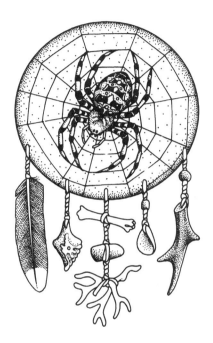

What is your relationship to the Great Creatrix Spider Mother? Spider is a weaving instructoress. Consider the web. What is the web of the life you have spun? You may wish to draw your personal web. What is caught in it? What is it you have to do in everyday reality to make your personal web strong? Perhaps some reweaving work is necessary. Are you willing to do the work? These are some of the questions you may want to consider before writing in your journal.

Spider
Mother sits
at the center
of the
universe. So
do you.

*What is
caught in
your web?*

*Spider is the
mistress
of nets.*

_____
_____
_____
_____
_____
_____
_____
_____
_____
_____
_____
_____
_____
_____
_____
_____
_____
_____
_____
_____
_____
_____
_____
_____
_____
_____
_____
_____
_____
_____
_____
_____
_____
_____
_____
_____

_Where are
the flaws in
your web
and how can
you mend
them?_

The web is of your own creation.

44
Hummingbird

JOY

Each day, Hummingbird gives us a choice. You can go to the Medicine Flower and choose to be happy, walk the Beauty Road, and be cheerful. You can also choose the opposite. Do you delight in your journey? Hummingbird asks you to explore joy and take your sorrow to a higher vibration. Use your journal to record what makes you happy. Use it to explore your sadness. Try to discover if the cause of your happiness is internal or external. Then call on Hummingbird's medicine to drink the sweet nectar of life.

*Break the
mask of
sorrow so
that you may
find the joy
hidden
within.*

Humming-bird calls to us for a celebration.

*Humming-
bird asks you
to consider
your spiritual
food.*

_We have joy
when there
are no
distractions,
no
confusions.
Joy is now._

Our Precious
Lady of the
Flowers,
Humming-
bird, teaches
the long
drink from
the sweetness
of life.

45
Blue Heron

SELF–REFLECTION

Behind logic is a mystery which cannot be understood by ordinary means. Blue Heron's flight is toward that discovery. She knows the reflective surfaces of the water world. Blue Heron has self-knowledge. The Great Blue Heron knows exactly when to act. She is elegant and essential. She knows that less is more. Through her movement, you witness her power to mirror her highest self in action. See if you can capture your limitless self and your capacity to create a miracle.

*Blue Heron
is keeper of
the mysteries
beneath the
surface.*

_Let the tiny
Blue Heron
show you
how she
breaks her
shell with
the tip of her
bill and
how, through
tireless effort,
she is free._

Blue Heron says, "My medicine is a mirror only if you are honest."

_____
_____
_____
_____
_____
_____
_____
_____
_____
_____
_____
_____
_____
_____
_____
_____
_____
_____
_____
_____
_____
_____
_____
_____
_____
_____
_____
_____
_____
_____
_____
_____
_____

Though difficult to realize, we can learn to enter Blue Heron's power.

*Grandmother
Blue Heron
is the perfect
actualization
of nothing
more or
nothing less
to do.*

46
Raccoon

GENEROUS PROTECTOR

Raccoon has a generous and loving spirit and knows how to share, especially with her family. She generously shares her material and spiritual goodies. She reads the signs and always knows what has happened. She is a guide and a protector. Raccoon has many powerful medicines. You may want to consider in your journal pages how you can give protection to those you love and care about. Make a will. Set up a trust fund. Do what you can for others who look to you for aid and comfort.

*Raccoon has
the ability
to show you
the proper
direction.*

_____
_____
_____
_____
_____
_____
_____
_____
_____
_____
_____
_____
_____
_____
_____
_____
_____
_____
_____
_____
_____
_____
_____
_____
_____
_____
_____
_____
_____
_____
_____

If you feel you have lost a part of your soul, Raccoon is the ally to help you find it.

*If you need
protection,
invoke the
spirit of
Raccoon.
Then be
decisive and
self-reliant.*

_____
_____
_____
_____
_____
_____
_____
_____
_____
_____
_____
_____
_____
_____
_____
_____
_____
_____
_____
_____
_____
_____
_____
_____
_____
_____
_____
_____
_____
_____
_____

Raccoon challenges you to find the new way out of difficulty. It is not often a straight line.

When you travel, ask Raccoon to protect you. She knows each step is the destination itself.

47
Prairie Dog

RETREAT

There are powers that bind us to institutions and ways of being that we intuitively know are archaic, demeaning, and threatening to our survival. When seeking to treat deep spiritual maladies that lead to mental unease and disease, take a lesson from Prairie Dog. Do yourself a favor: Retreat. Retreat to reharmonize with your perfect inner stillness. Retreat when life becomes an unbearable burden and there is no end to your suffering. Re-*treat,* accent on *treat.* Let that be the operative word. Treat yourself with kindness.

*Prairie Dog
often plays
the sun
game. When
Eagle's
shadow falls
on the ground
from above,
Prairie Dog
goes on
retreat.*

Take Prairie Dog's advice— disappear every day for fifteen minutes.

Prairie Dog is an urbanite. Prairie Dog villages stretch for hundreds of miles.

*To learn
unknown
parts of
yourself,
consider
Prairie Dog.
She digs into
the lower
world and
kicks up the
dirt to the
surface.*

*Take counsel
with Prairie
Dog. Let her
show you
the inner
labyrinths
of Earth's
medicine.*

48
Wild Boar

CONFRONTATION

Wild Boar gives warning about a person or problem that needs to be dealt with immediately, or the situation could get out of hand and grow to enormous proportions. We all have tasks that we don't want to do, but must. Wild Boar gives you the courage to confront the power to cut yourself free from your attachments to old ways of being. Wild Boar is a warrior with strong inner drives to face any threat or problem. He is brave in confronting the adversary in a direct and simple way. He is the sudden and realized warrior who leads the fight against those who threaten. Right now, confront your journal.

When Wild
Boar starts
rooting
around, it
takes bravery
to confront
him. Watch
out. He
knows how
to maneuver
and come at
you fast. He
has a shrill
war cry.

_Wild Boar
senses
weakness.
He's ruthless.
He's
dangerous,
cunning,
and bold._

Wild Boar is a harsh teacher. He forces you to confront whatever is necessary with clear intent.

_____

There are times we must stand up and be fearless.

*Wild Boar
teaches
responsibility
and the
ability to
respond to
problems
immediately.*

49
Salmon

WISDOM/INNER KNOWING

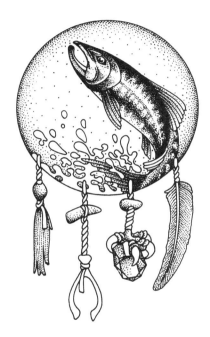

Salmon reveals many beautiful faces of wisdom. Salmon seeks the original source. She is free of confusion and error. Seeking wisdom is often lonely. The best guide is inner knowing. There are few resting places along the way. The way is perilous and requires unceasing effort and a willingness to sacrifice. Sink or swim. Return to your truth or drown. Your very cells know this. Trust your inner knowing. Let Salmon dive you deep into living waters.

*Wisdom is
the courage
to face
yourself and
your false
beliefs—to
swim against
the currents
of the
moment.*

Wise
Salmon
understands
her mission.

Old Mother
Salmon
returns to the
place of her
creation—the
place where
she first met
with Creator
who told her,
"Before your
death, come
back here
and lay
your eggs."

There is no
expectation
of reward in
Salmon's
wisdom.

*Salmon
seeks the
beginning,
where going
forward
becomes a
returning
to self-
knowledge.*

50
Alligator

INTEGRATION

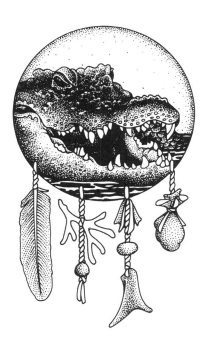

Alligator is the old one, the ancient one who keeps forgotten memories. The world is in her mouth, as well as many other universes and realities. Alligator realizes mystic unity through the powers of integration. Alligator demands that we be vigilant, awake, and fully alive. Her integrative lesson is that all of life is interdependent. She has the ability to realign her spirit by integrating the new. List several things you want to pull into your consciousness. Submerge and let them sink in.

*Alligators are
the precious
ones, the
pure ones,
integrating
and accepting
of all
dimensions.*

Alligator integrates the ebb and flow of being.

*Alligator's
medicine
glides you
through the
opening
between two
worlds.*

Waters are changed in the mysterious swamps and bayous. This world belongs to Alligator.

*Alligator
reminds you
to use your
energy to
integrate and
manifest the
greatest good.*

51
Jaguar
INTEGRITY/IMPECCABILITY

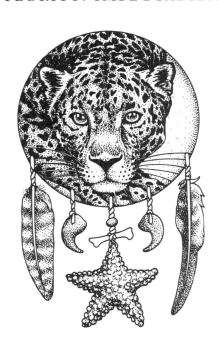

Eyes of Jaguar pierce with unshakable force. She can show many faces, but she is incapable of lying. Jaguar has no internal conflict. Always impeccable, integrity is her exact essence, her distinct nature. If you are courting Jaguar for power, she exacts total commitment. There is a circle at your feet. That circle belongs to you. It's yours and no one else's. Jaguar demands that you put integrity and impeccability inside your personal circle. Be impeccable in word, deed, and thought. Power will emanate from you and your medicine will be unmistakable.

*She is an
unfailing
ally.*

The House
of Jaguar
holds the
knowledge of
prophecy.
No wonder
Jaguar guards
the entrance
to the next
world.

*Impeccability
is not
rigidity.*

_If you feel
yourself
slipping
away from
your ideal,
call on Jaguar
medicine and
she will direct
you back._

Jaguar escorts
the high
initiate into
the borning
world—the
next great
age of
creation.

52
Black Panther

EMBRACING THE UNKNOWN

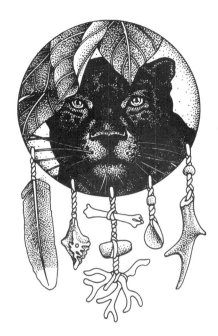

Black Panther shows you how to get out of your own way—to disappear. She gives you the medicine to walk into the jaws of the unknown and be swallowed by it. Black Panther does not resist the unfathomable, the unknowable. It is difficult to face the unknown. Yet one must accept what it brings. Black Panther teaches that the unknown is not beyond comprehension. The unknown is right in front of you, waiting to be embraced.

Pounce!
Seize the
unknown by
the scruff of
the neck.

*She is the
beautiful
dark one, the
mysterious
one. She
understands
and teaches
us the
walkway
to the
unknown.*

*Be patient
and study
Night's
medicine.
The
unknown
eventually
falls into the
moonlight.*

Accept the unknown as a gift, for often it is the perfect blessing.

*Revel in
the power
of your
premonitions
like the great
black cat.
Go with
confidence
and know
you will find
your answer.*

SACRED TECHNOLOGY ON THE WHEEL
OF DESTRUCTION AND CREATION

Long ago, the medicine wheel was seen as the cosmic serpent biting its tail and it encircled the universe. It was the lodge of new life of the sun dance. It was the medicine circle, the holy circle. It was the *inipe* lodge of purification. It was the source within the source. Some called it the Circle of Life, the Ancestor Circle of many generations, Hub of Being, Hoop of Creation, Ring of Spirit, Life's Map, Magic Circle, and so on. There are many ways to describe the Sacred Wheel and the points of meaning of the directions.

The cardinal points East, South, West and North are said to be bearer positions. The inner-cardinal points Southeast, Southwest, Northwest and Northeast are said to be embracer positions.

There is an easy way to extract information from the Medicine Wheel. Personify it. This is what the wheel would look like if a person stood at each of the directions. In the East stands the Contrary—the Sacred Clown. In the Southeast stands the Medicine Man or Medicine Woman or both. In the South stands the Hunter-Warrior. In the Southwest stands the Politician. In the West is the Witch or Sorcerer. In the Northwest is the Judge. In the North is the Old Philosopher. In the Northeast is the Seer or Prophet. And in the Center is the Higher Self.

When doing a Medicine Card reading, ask each persona at these positions for their help and guidance in interpreting a card. Go within yourself and ask the persona to show you, signify or symbolize to you the information each is willing to share. It may take practice, but sooner or later the process will bear fruit.

Here are some examples to illuminate the encounters you have as you circumnavigate the Sacred Wheel. The Contrary stands in the East and advises about the paradoxical nature of the wheel you have entered. The Contrary turns your question back on itself and gives a backward or opposite answer.

The Medicine Man or Medicine Woman in the embracer position of the Southeast does rituals and ceremonies to heal you and advises you on matters of personal power.

The Hunter-Warrior in the South teaches you about the hunt and war trails, advises you about weapons, and shows you the strength and weakness of your prey.

The Politician in the Southwest advises you on how to use the situation for your personal gain and how to triumph over others who are competing for the same goal. Ask the Politician how to get the loot.

In the West is the Witch or Sorcerer. Ask the Witch or Sorcerer what is hidden in your question or problem and about your own and other's true motives.

In the Northwest is the Judge. Ask the Judge about rules and regulations and about standards of behavior. Ask the judge to critique your situation with a neutral eye and heart.

In the North is the Old Philosopher who draws from the well of life's long memory. Expect deep and profound answers from the Philosopher.

The Seer or Prophet is in the Northeast. Ask the Seer or Prophet about the spiritual aspects of a question—the good way, the holy way.

In the Center, warm your hands on the fires of the Higher Self. Take into account your ancestors and seven future generations in this position and seek your own best counsel.

Gradually increase your subjective and objective familiarity with the sacred teachings of the Medicine Wheel. Do meditations facing the exact compass point of each of the cardinal and inner-cardinal directions. Take note of their subtle energy. Note how you feel. Which directions make you feel comfortable? Which direction stimulates you? Do you feel diminished in any certain direction? If so, why? Develop a clearer perception of each direction and become more sensitive to each one. Record your experiences in your journal.

East

Entering the Gate Card: This is the bearing position of the sun nourished East. The East represents illumination. It is the place of our most noble convictions. Since it is a place of giving birth, there is also the possibility of trauma, but this is not its main message. Spiritual traditions the world over teach us that the approach to enlightenment can be dangerous and cause insanity or even death if we are not prepared to meet effulgent light. Therefore, the East is a delicate transition direction. True light burns through us. It teaches we must learn not to have attachments, to be transparent. If we learn to let go of our ego investment within the question, we can accept perfect revelation. Remember that East teaches that a beginning is also an ending.

Southeast

Gathering Power Card: This is an embracer position. It is the position of personal power. It holds much information about your present abilities. It is the position of the white star who is said to be the mother of the first humans—moon being the midwife. This mother was supported by the constellations bear, panther, wild cat, wolf, and a group of serpent stars.

The Gathering of Power position represents relationships and guidance from our teachers and ancestors. This direction represents inner road maps or guides—genetic information at a cellular level. Southeast carries the amusement of life and its vicissitudes—a pleasant and knowing smile. It is the place of the aesthete—a place of elegance and beauty. The concern here is personal power and the card suggests how to get it.

South

Land of Giants Card: Trust as well as innocence is here in the South. This is the territory of the child living in a land of grown-ups—adults. Later in life we must face other kinds of giants. Often it is giants who are our enemy, so we must learn how to fight and vanquish them in an honorable way. The position often speaks of the naiveté of a child. It is the greening position.

The South speaks of consensus. The child must become socialized and battle their way into consensus reality. The child must learn to stalk their vision. Here we ask about the successful hunt. What are we stalking and hunting and how can we track and kill it? Do we have the proper weapons? If not, how can we obtain them? The South speaks of the game of life and suggests our strengths in playing it. It speaks of the physical world and collective consciousness.

Southwest

Stratagem Card: Southwest is the place to define possible accomplishments based on present circumstances. It is the place of refined skills of the adroit manipulator. It questions your ideals and degree of commitment. It often reveals your level of involvement with the problem, process, or question. It may reference obstacles you are meeting. It may reveal the mood that surrounds the question. Look here for advice on finances and suggestions on how to get the loot or how to meet a debt repayment. Seek guidance here for how to influence any situation.

West

Looks-within Card: West is the place of introspection. Just as Bear often enters her winter cave backwards, this card position often means to carefully consider the past. West is the position of introspection, the sacred hibernaculum. It is the place of the deepest contemplation and inner knowing. Here are our dreams and visions. This direction represents our goals and ambitions. The understanding of our death is the West and it is the place of acknowledgment of our death. It is the sacrificial position, the place of the adult. This position may bring intuitive aspects of the West as well as enhanced creativity. Look to this card for understanding of your innermost nature.

Northwest

Critic Card: Here in the Northwest is the place of judgment, that moment between thinking and doing, that moment before acceptance or negation. Look here for suggestions on how to break or enforce laws you have set for yourself. It is a place to enlarge or reduce choices. Look here for power to escape any sort of entrapment. Northwest is the place of sacred images and sacred laws. Human law is often unjust. Here may also manifest dark and moral rules and laws of denial. It can be a place of vengeance. This card should be examined to define the judgments of others as well as our own.

North

Circumspection Card: North is the place of wisdom and spirit. It is identified with the greater intellect. Look here for aids to logic. This card may suggest ways to enhance reasoning power or solve intellectual quandaries. North is also the place of complete wisdom. We seek the gifts of spirit to be given in wisdom. Wisdom comes from living a long life and experiencing life's full circle. Look to this card to determine the wisest path and for a suggestion of the outcome of events. If your question has a material aspect, remember the law that matter follows spirit.

Northeast

Oracular Card: Look to this card to resolve issues in a positive manner. Northeast is the place of understanding the spiritual principles in all questions. It speaks of the end of a cycle. It speaks of not getting stuck in ambition or materialism. It speaks of surrender, trust, faith, and joy in the next round of being. Look to this sacred space to see designs, patterns, and choreography of events. Here one may experience the cosmic dance of creation—around and around we go in the ceremonial circle of life. The Great Mysterious has bidden us to dance, to hear the song of a new dawn, and recover the reverence within us. The wind swirls and the clouds are pregnant with rain. There is lightning on the mountaintop as we ready ourselves to meet the Spirit of Spirits.

center

Umbilicus Card: There is a saying, "All things go to the center, to the remembering pole—to the tree, to the fire, to power." This is the place of true magic for it is here that we find another dimension in clear fact. We find ourselves.

Standing at the remembering pole or tree is standing in a timeless place. When we concern ourselves with matters that lie outside ourselves, we have lost focus. Looking outward alienates us from the centering place. Just as the council fire burns in the center of the tipi, and the heated stones are in center of the *inipi* lodge, so does the fire of High Self burn in our centering place.

To dance around the central fire is to dance around the heart of the universe. Here is the seat of your highest ideals and how they might manifest themselves. Look at this position for the objectivity and fairness of the balanced whole. Look to this card to suggest the stalk that carries the leaves of the other directions. There is a place within you that leads to all the points of the compass—a place that holds completion. That is the power of this position.

SEVEN CEREMONIES TO RESOLVE
CONFLICT BETWEEN TWO PEOPLE

He was born on a travois leaving the Little Big Horn battlefield. His name was Willis Medicine Bull, and he was one of the last living Cheyenne Peace Chiefs. I had the honor of knowing him when I lived in Lame Deer, Montana. He would never speak English even though I suspected he understood the language. He was a wise and holy man. I owe the knowledge on which the following ceremonies are based to him. I dedicate this understanding of conflict resolution to his memory and the memory of all the Peace Chiefs before him.

The President of the United States would do well to have a Peace Chief on his Cabinet. Peace Chiefs were analogous to Bodhisattvas. They were evolved, compassionate, and realized. They were spiritual leaders. They were pacific. *Their vow was to never harm any living being and never speak ill of another.* Their path was the path of peace. Most of the time they were elders but not always. Peace Chiefs held a vision of a better world here upon our Motherworld. They radiated love. They were tolerant. They were in accord with humanity and all of creation. Their words, which they seldom spoke, carried much weight. Spiritually, their word was the law.

These ceremonies and the Medicine Card usage are based on the Council of Peace Chiefs of the Plains People. Peace Chiefs taught that conflicts are sacred and must be understood as separation from the Oneness of creation. Their motto was always, "Let people both profit from the conflict and gain in spiritual understanding." Remember that long ago conflicts that threatened tribal unity were presented to the Peace Chiefs. The gathering of these wise and knowing Chiefs was in itself an admonition not to be petty or cynical. Their very presence was an incentive to work for a solution to all the issues.

Conflict exists. It is germane to life. Conflict, of one kind or another, lurks deep within us and often manifests outward into consensus reality. What is my spiritual path? How can I make some money? How can I resolve such-and-so situation? How can I deal with the death of a loved one? How can I attract a soul mate or partner into my life? People ask the Medicine Cards for answers. They call upon hidden or not-so-hidden powers of the cosmos for guidance. They turn to the living bio-computer of Earth itself for subtle nudges to guide them in their struggles. When we are not at peace with ourselves, we are in conflict.

There are other kinds of conflict as well, between people, special interest groups, communities, and nations. Conflict always stems from the individual conflict within one person. It may then become the consciousness of all. One person may set a ripple of conflict that engulfs the planet. Without love and respect for each other there will always be conflict. It is best to diminish conflict whenever possible.

This method of settling differences is derived from a historical tribal culture very different from our own, and it may not completely satisfy your needs. Remember two dogs and a bone. Bones are not easily divided. Not all conflict can be resolved. Issues of sex, money, and other materialistic matters; issues of drug, alcohol, and other addictions; issues of dominance, authority and control; all these run deep in Western culture. Often our society begets combative and non-cooperative modes of behavior. Hostility, intolerance, and rigidity are fostered and cloud our perceptions. We are conditioned to conform to cultural biases. Our responses to conflict reflect this hidebound condition.

If you are in conflict with another person, go before the Chiefs. Give the Peace Chiefs the opportunity to bring about positive closure. If this method doesn't work, at least both parties will have agreed to resolve their conflict in an honorable way. You can still agree to disagree forever. You can choose to go in separate directions with new respect for the other party.

Choose to live with a new solution. These are simple ceremonies, but for those who are unfamiliar with ritual methods, consult literature on the subject before doing them. Rituals are sacred technology. Consider rituals as either the subtle manipulation of natural forces or the intelligent use of creative metaphor. A ritual is a conduit for spiritual energy to come to your aid.

The design of these ceremonies and rituals is up to you. However, the seven ceremonies must be performed in sequence. The most important aspect of any ritual is focused and clear intention. When two people have complete agreement there is synergy—a power many times stronger than that of a single individual. I recommended that you include at least some of the following during each of the seven ceremonies:

Do fasting.

Do tobacco prayer ties.

Do sweat lodge or some other form of cleansing.

Wear sacred garments or some special clothing.

Prepare a space that exists "outside" of the world where the conflict began. The space should be free of noise and interruptions.

Make a circle.

Call in the powers of the four directions.

Acknowledge the elements air, fire, earth, and water.

Burn sage, cedar, sweetgrass, or fragrant incense.

Use an altar. Many traditional altars are placed in the west but you may situate your personal altar in another direction. This is perfectly acceptable.

Include religious icons or spiritual symbols in the performance of your ritual.

Include special objects such as feathers, fans, stones, knives, arrows, spirit bundles, or other magical items.

Burn candles.

Drum, rattle, or sing a song.

Say prayers.

Invoke spirits, angels, or other non-ordinary helpers.

Invoke the spirits of animal guides and protectors.

Give offerings to your ancestors and call for their presence, their guidance, and their blessing.

Do a closing ritual.

Show gratitude by thanking all the known and unknown dimensions and powers.

Ceremonies create a fusion point and are at the crossroads of evolution and involution. It is the in-between place where two realities become one. Every incursion into spiritual planes is serious. The decision to perform these ceremonies cannot be taken lightly. The meaning and purpose of the Seven Ceremonies is to reaffirm your responsibility to the complexity of the whole of life by coming to terms with individual conflict.

Ceremony One

CONFLAGRATION: THE HEART OF FIRE

A fire has broken out in the village. Conflict often denotes compulsive, uncontrolled behavior. Pain, anger, and revulsion run unchecked. One or both parties to the conflict are behaving compulsively and are in a lock. Each must look for ways to break the chains of conflict and be free. The fire of conflict must first be banked, slowed, and managed. To do this, each must acknowledge and accept responsibility for their role. Each has chosen his or her responses and reactions. Each has chosen for themselves the degree of anger or pain engendered by the conflict. Now each must lay down judgment and seek to remedy the situation. Both must agree to resolve the conflict for the good of all concerned. Once this is determined, each person must do prayers and ritual to seek guidance about the conflict. Select a Medicine Card and note all details for later consideration.

Ceremony Two

BANKING THE FIRE: REMOVING THE ARROW
FROM THE BOWSTRING

Both parties must do their utmost to extinguish the negative emotions generated by the conflict. After taking responsibility for your state of being, it becomes possible to take responsible action on your own behalf. You must deal with your bruised ego, pain, anger or other mental anguish. It is important to put emotions behind you. Do not try to limit them. Strive to relocate them. Put your emotions behind you.

Peace Chiefs teach that emotions are spatial, that is, located in space. Over time, the locus shifts. The following ritual is offered to accelerate a natural process. Here are its most essential aspects. Each party to the conflict must do the ceremony separately and away from the other party. First, obtain a small stone, the heavier the better. Ask the stone for permission to use it in your ritual. Hold the stone in your right hand. Ask the stone to accept your feelings generated by the conflict. Put all your emotions caused by the conflict into the stone—any pain, anger, or any other negative emotion. Then, take the stone to a tree and bury it. Thank the stone, earth, and tree for helping you. Leave. As you walk away from the site, visualize the emotion as being behind you. This is not simply a mental trick. When emotions are in the past, that is exactly where they are—passed. Your emotions are no longer hanging in front and goading you—being fed from the fires of your passion and becoming more and more monstrous. It's important to visualize the relocation of your emotions as being behind you. Never deal with the emotions as being in front of you again.

After the ritual, select a Medicine Card to bind it. Write of the process in your journal.

ceremony Three

BUILDING THE NEW FIRE: BRINGING THE SACRED ARROWS
TO THE CEREMONIAL TREATY GROUNDS

The two people in conflict meet in an agreed-upon place. Choose a place of
power that reflects the peaceful spirit you are seeking. If possible, choose a natural setting near a lake or mountain. Choose a place of beauty and solitude. The
territory must be neutral where neither person owns the space.

The two people sit across from each other, on the ground, floor, or at a table.
A silent prayer is offered. Next, a small gift is exchanged, an offering of peace if
only for the time being. This is more than a token. It represents the sharing of
the pipe. It represents greater community—the interrelatedness and interdepen-
dency of all of life. It is acknowledgment that sacred connectedness is influenced
by our decisions. The process begins in peace in order that it may be concluded
in peace. Each person selects a random Medicine Card. This card suggests what
to consider as the journey of resolution begins. This should be recorded in your
journal as well as the card selected and the gifts exchanged.

Ceremony Four

Begin with a joint ceremony. Scout the conflict by writing it down. This is your chance to state your version of the conflict. Describe the conflict and everything you know about it. Make the description as detailed as possible. There is no time constraint here. Take as long as necessary. Select a Medicine Card and record it. Then, exchange journals. Without discussion, study and internalize the position of the other person. Silence is maintained until the next ceremony.

Ceremony Five

ASHING THE COALS: SHOOTING THE CONTRARY ARROWS

A contrary arrow is gnarled, twisted, and incapable of hurting anyone.

The contrary plays a sacred role in tribal life. A contrary balances opposites. They own the power of Lightning. A contrary cannot be touched by anyone. To do so is to risk the striking power of the Lightning lance. The contrary teaches of the hidden death within all living forms and the hidden life within all dead forms.

The contrary takes ordinary behavior and stands it on its head. He does everything backwards—he runs backward when others walk forward. Good-bye is hello. He walks, talks, and always acts contrary. His world is the reverse of ours. Hot is cold. Day is night.

The contrary has the power to blind one with the inverse, giving one a sudden burst of power to see the opposite contained in every situation. Often hilariously funny, contrary medicine is compounded absurdity. The intent is never to harm.

The powerful spirit of the contrary is invoked for the fifth ceremony. Contrary ceremonies are an invitation to understanding and wholeness—a leaping backward to non-separation. They produce an energy that demolishes lies and leads to a higher truth.

This ceremony begins backward with each person entering the space backward. Places are exchanged. Roles are reversed. Each person in turn must state the contrary position—the position of the other person. This is not symbolic of walking in the moccasins of the other person. It is a conversion of energy. One must do their utmost to touch with the soul of the other and to experience the other's being and point of view.

Afterward, both people leave the space backward. Pull a Medicine Card and consider its meaning in light of what has happened to you. Note everything in your journal.

Again, silence is maintained until the sixth ceremony.

Ceremony Six

Do a ritual for centering and clarity.

Empty your mind. List all possible solutions to your conflict. It doesn't matter how diverse or even contradictory the solutions might be. No judgment. Light or dark, list them. Write anything that comes to mind as a solution even though it makes no logical sense. Push the envelope further. Select a Medicine Card and follow the animal's trail and see where it leads. Then leave the space. Go off alone and relax. Ask Higher Power for one more solution.

Return to the space and note what has transpired in your journal. Do a closing ritual.

Ceremony Seven

SCATTERING THE ASHES FOREVER: BREAKING THE ARROW

Walk into this ceremony knowing that it brings completion. Do a ritual opening of the ceremony. Consider the generations that will follow you. Pray for the children to come and the children's children. Remember, nothing should be done that will harm children.

Your destination is resolution. Ask the animal powers to show you your path and select a Medicine Card. Call upon the medicine to inform the ceremony.

You have experienced conflict. The medicine wheels teach that you are a microcosm within the macrocosm. You represent the universe, and the universe represents you. When you are in conflict, you extend conflict into the totality of being. Now, extend your presence and become one with the solution.

Attention must be directed to resolution. Tolerance and the spirit of compromise contribute to a positive outcome. Seek ways of cooperation. Find solutions. Discuss each and every idea. Take responsibility. Each person must agree on the solution and abide by it. Write it down in language you both understand and read it to each other. Acknowledge that there is agreement.

This breaks the arrow of conflict.

Conclude the ceremony.

Within four days, share your solution with one other person. This could be a minister, priest, rabbi, elder, social worker, counselor, medicine person or any person recognized for their spiritual qualities.

When a resolution was arrived at before the gathering of Peace Chiefs, a solemn oath was taken. To break one's word, was to insult all of Great Mystery's gifts. The Peace Chiefs touched the people with an eagle feather and told them to walk the path of peace.

Notes on Card Readings and Animal Encounters